DINOSAUR DISCOVERY ACTIVITY BOOK

by Brett Ortler

illustrations by Scott Rolfs

Minneapolis, Minnesota

AUTHOR'S NOTE

There are many different dinosaurs—over a thousand kinds. Many more are still waiting to be discovered. Even some of the most famous dinosaurs can still be surprising. For example, did you know there's more than one kind (or species) of Triceratops? Each species can be pretty different in size and weight from other species. This means that talking about a dinosaur's size or weight isn't always easy. The information I've listed about each species is for the largest it might have been. These differences are what make dinosaurs so interesting. With that said, I hope you enjoy this book as much as I enjoyed writing it.

DEDICATION

To Oliver, Violet, and Charlie, my favorite dinosaur fans.

Edited by Ryan Jacobson
Book design and cover design by Ryan Jacobson

Special thanks to Jon Kramer for fact-checking

Word find puzzles made at www.puzzle-maker.com
Maze puzzles from Shutterstock.com

Copyright 2015 by Brett Ortler
Published by Lake 7 Creative, LLC
Minneapolis, MN 55412
www.lake7creative.com

ISBN: 978-1-940647-15-9

WHAT ARE DINOSAURS?

Dinosaurs are reptiles that lived long ago. From the meat-eating Tyrannosaurus Rex to the plant-eating Brachiosaurus, there were many different dinosaurs. They had a lot of different features, too: horns, claws, feathers, and even armor.

The dinosaurs went extinct (died out) about 65 million years ago. This probably happened because a large asteroid hit Earth. Not every creature died, though. __ __ __ __ __ were one group that lived.

Scientists now know that __ __ __ __ __ are related to dinosaurs. This means you don't need to go back in time to see dinosaurs. Just look out the window!

ACTIVITY: Connect the dots below to see which common animals are related to dinosaurs. Then fill in the blanks above.

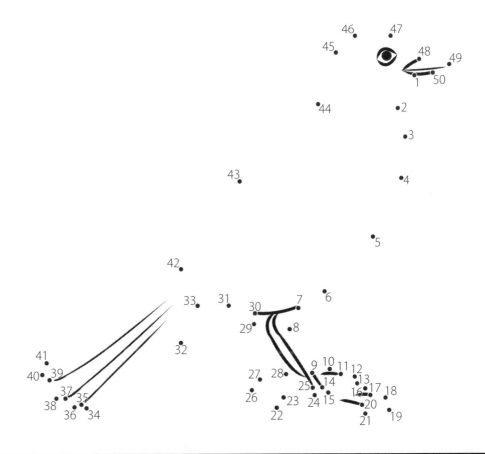

 Don't believe it? Before you say, "No way," think about this: Dinosaurs laid eggs like birds. They made nests like birds. Some dinosaurs even had feathers. Plus, dinosaur bones are a lot like bird bones.

DINOSAUR TIMELINE

The Earth is more than 4.5 billion years old. Dinosaurs first appeared about 251 million years ago. They lived for a long time, until about 65 million years ago. (Yes, dinosaurs were around for about 186 million years! Humans have only been here for about two million years.)

It can get confusing to think about millions of years. So scientists talk about specific time periods. The age of dinosaurs—all 186 million years—is called the **MESOZOIC ERA** (*mez-oh-zoe-ick air-uh*).

The Mesozoic Era is broken into three smaller time periods:

1. **TRIASSIC PERIOD** (*tri-as-ick peer-ee-ud*): 251–199 million years ago

2. **JURASSIC PERIOD** (*jer-as-ick peer-ee-ud*): 199–145 million years ago

3. **CRETACEOUS PERIOD** (*cruh-tae-shuss peer-ee-ud*): 145–65 million years ago

Eoraptor
235–228 million
years ago

Triassic Period

Jurassic Period

Plateosaurus
222–215 million
years ago

Not all dinosaurs lived at the same time. For example, the Stegosaurus lived in the late Jurassic Period, but the Tyrannosaurus Rex lived in the late Cretaceous Period. So two of the most famous dinosaur species never even met!

ACTIVITY: Color the dinosaurs shown on the timeline below. Which of these dinosaurs could the Tyrannosaurus Rex have eaten? How do you know?

_____

_____

_____

_____

_____

Stegosaurus
157–150 million
years ago

Tyrannosaurus Rex
67–66 million
years ago

Cretaceous Period

Brachiosaurus
156–146 million
years ago

Triceratops
68–65 million
years ago

DINOSAUR GROUPS

There are more than 1,000 kinds of dinosaurs. Scientists organize them into two main groups:

1. **SAURISCHIA** (*soar-ish-ee-uh*)

2. **ORNITHISCHIA** (*or-nith-ish-ee-uh*)

What's the difference between the two groups? It might sound strange, but one of the biggest differences is in the hips. Both groups of dinosaurs have the same number and types of hip bones, but their hip bones are put together differently. Take a look:

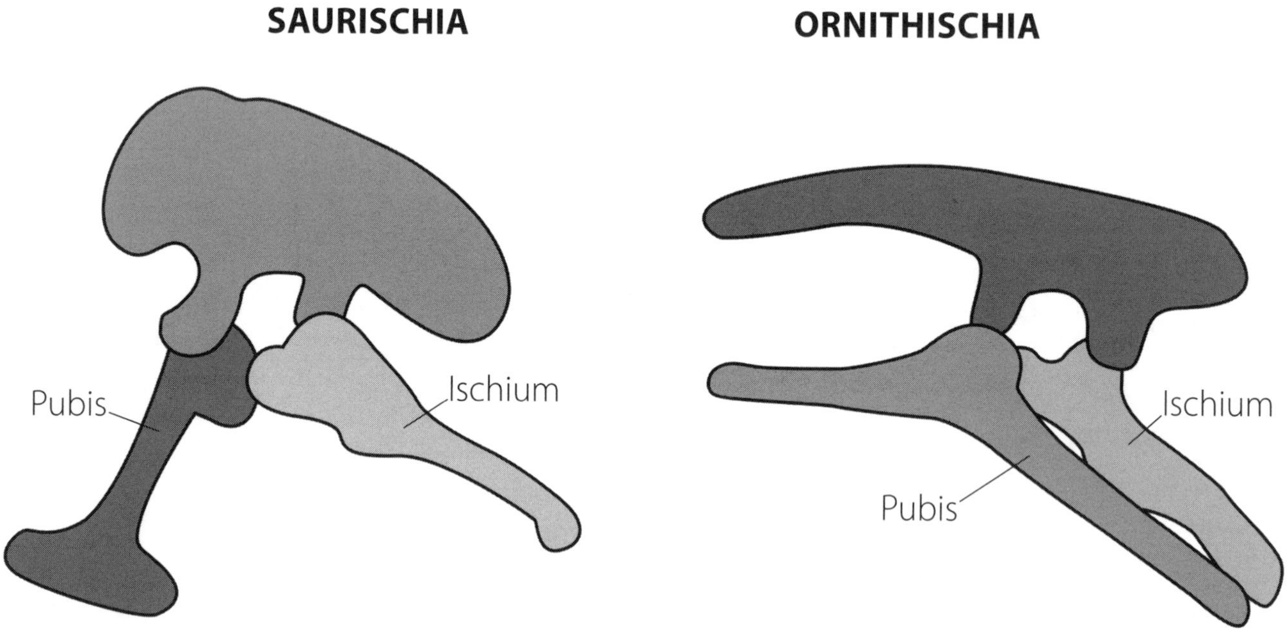

SAURISCHIA   **ORNITHISCHIA**

Pubis   Ischium   Ischium   Pubis

Each of the two main groups is broken down into a number of other groups. Here are a few examples:

SAURISCHIA

Theropods (includes Tyrannosaurus Rex)

Sauropods (includes Brachiosaurus)

ORNITHISCHIA

Ceratopsians (includes Triceratops)

Ankylosaurs (includes Ankylosaurus)

Stegosaurs (includes Stegosaurus)

Ornithopods (includes Iguanodon)

DINOSAUR MATCHING

Read the information about Dinosaur Groups on page 6. Then match each of the dinosaurs below to the kind of dinosaur it was. One has been done for you.

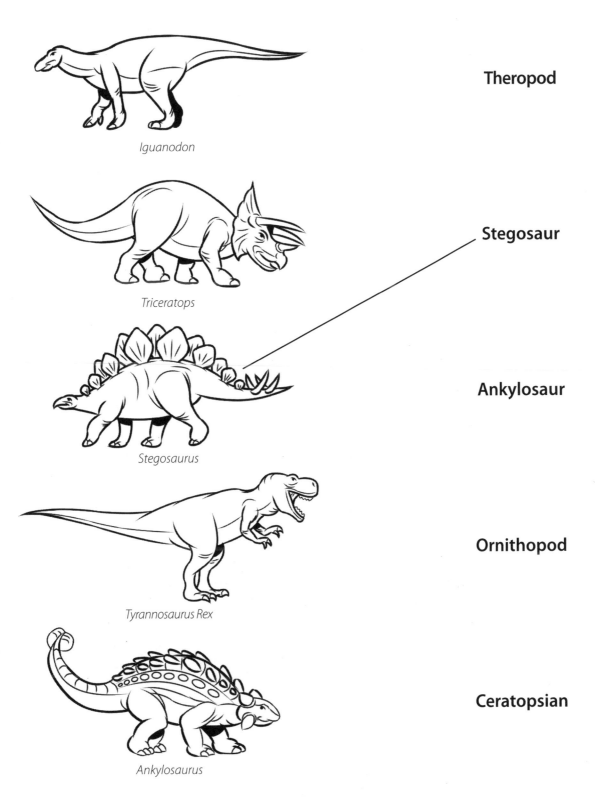

Iguanodon

Theropod

Triceratops

Stegosaur

Stegosaurus

Ankylosaur

Tyrannosaurus Rex

Ornithopod

Ankylosaurus

Ceratopsian

answers on page 62

TRIASSIC PERIOD

(251–199 million years ago)

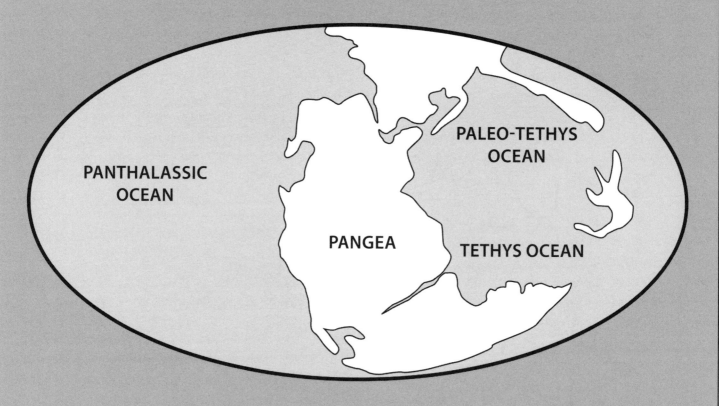

PALEO-TETHYS OCEAN

PANTHALASSIC OCEAN

PANGEA

TETHYS OCEAN

If you saw a picture of Earth during the Triassic Period, you might not know which planet it was. For one thing, the land was shaped differently. At the beginning of the Triassic, there was only one large mass of land, or continent, called Pangea.

Flowering plants didn't exist yet, so you'd never see a rose bush or an apple tree. Instead, the main plants were ferns and pine trees. The weather was warmer and drier than it is now, so there was no ice at the North Pole or the South Pole.

At the beginning of the Triassic Period, the land was very empty. It was there for any creatures that could survive. One group—the archosaurs (ark-oh-soars)— soon did. As they adapted, a new type of creature was born: the dinosaur.

TRIASSIC CROSSWORD

Solve the crossword puzzle below with information about the Triassic Period.

ACROSS

1. A relative to dinosaurs and crocodiles

3. Small predator from 230 million years ago

5. CHALLENGE: This dinosaur's name began with what food is served on

DOWN

2. One of the first turtle species

4. CHALLENGE: This kind of dry habitat was common during the Triassic Period

5. The massive supercontinent of the Triassic Period

BEFORE THE DINOSAURS

The first dinosaurs came from reptiles known as archosaurs (ark-oh-soars). It means "ruling reptiles." The name is a good fit because archosaurs came to rule the Triassic Period. There were many different kinds of archosaurs, like armored plant-eaters and meat-eating land animals. Some looked like huge crocodiles.

ACTIVITY: Archosaurs are no longer around, but some relatives of archosaurs still exist. Examples include crocodiles and birds. The creature above was a 15-foot-long, meat-eating archosaur. It was related to crocodiles. Use the code below to learn the name of this archosaur.

____ ____ ____ ____ ____ ____ ____ ____ ____ ____ ____ ____
16 18 5 19 20 15 19 21 3 8 21 19

1	2	3	4	5	6	7	8	9	10	11	12	13	14	15	16	17	18	19	20	21	22	23	24	25	26
A	B	C	D	E	F	G	H	I	J	K	L	M	N	O	P	Q	R	S	T	U	V	W	X	Y	Z

EORAPTOR (ee-oh-rap-tur)

The Eoraptor is one of the first known dinosaur species. Eoraptors lived about 230 million years ago. As far as dinosaurs go, they were pretty small: about three feet long and one foot tall. Eoraptors ate meat. They probably hunted smaller animals and ate meat from larger, already dead animals that they found.

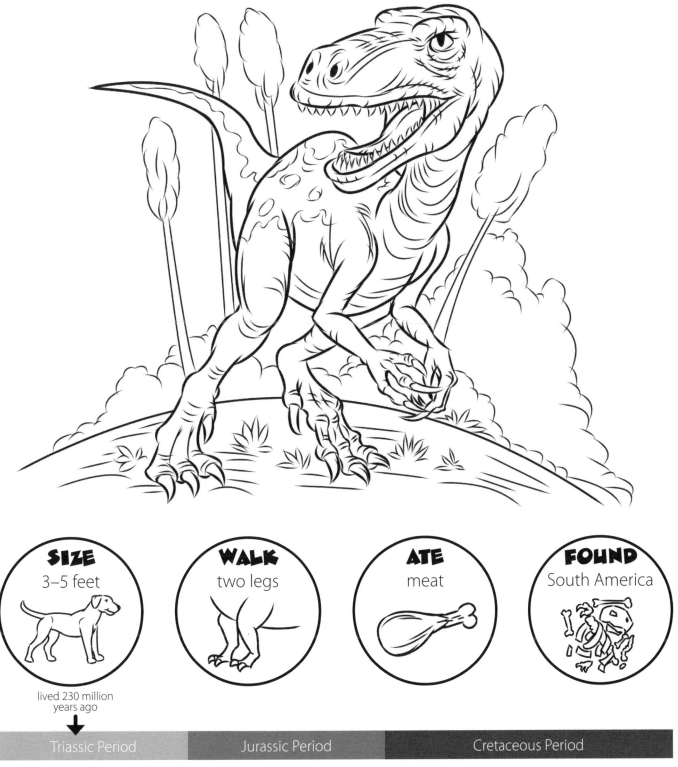

SIZE
3–5 feet

lived 230 million
years ago

WALK
two legs

ATE
meat

FOUND
South America

Triassic Period	Jurassic Period	Cretaceous Period

ODONTOCHELYS *(oh-don-toe-kell-iss)*

Odontochelys wasn't a dinosaur, but it's the oldest known relative of the turtle. The species was a lot different than turtles as we know them. Like turtles of today, it had a flat bottom part of the shell. It didn't have a rounded top half, though. Plus, while today's turtles have beaks, Odontochelys had teeth!

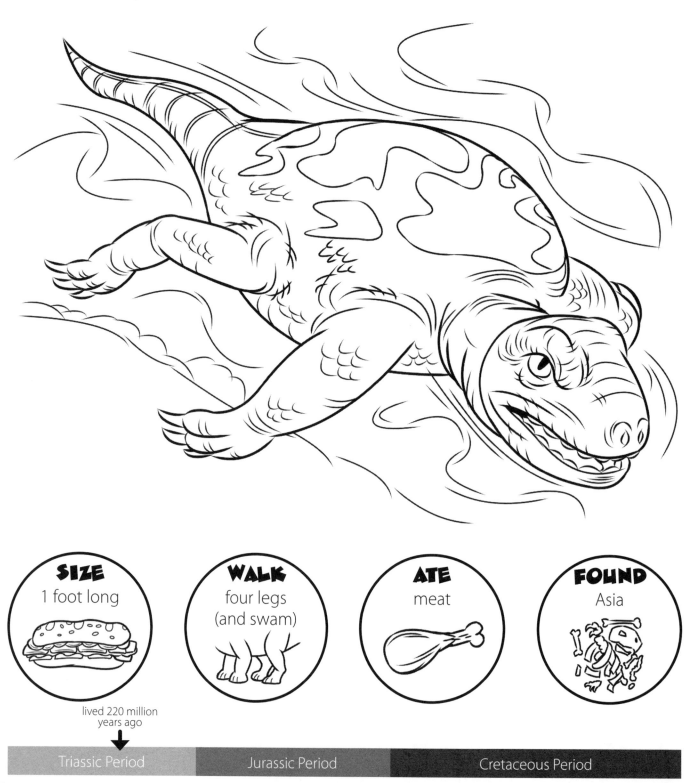

SIZE
1 foot long

lived 220 million years ago

WALK
four legs
(and swam)

ATE
meat

FOUND
Asia

| Triassic Period | Jurassic Period | Cretaceous Period |

DINOSAUR SIZES

Dinosaurs and other ancient animals came in many different shapes and sizes. Study the dinosaurs and other objects below. Rank them in size from smallest to largest. (The smallest will be number 1. The largest will be number 7.)

Car _____

Prestosuchus _____

Tyrannosaurus Rex _____

Eoraptor _____

Brachiosaurus _____

Elephant _____

Skyscraper _____

JURASSIC PERIOD

(199–145 million years ago)

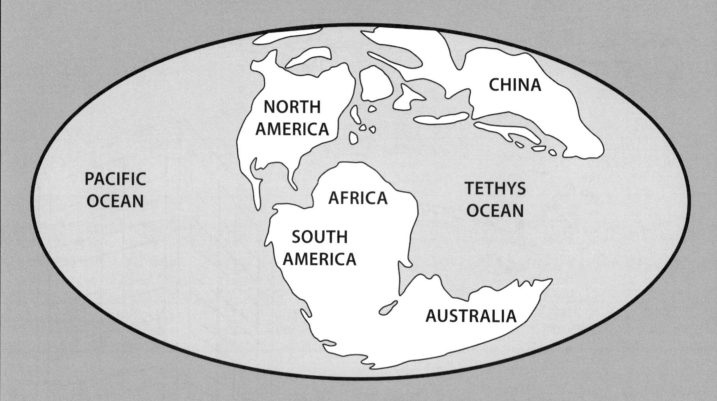

When you imagine the land of the dinosaurs, you probably think of the Jurassic Period. It was a warm, wet, and often swampy place. Much of the land was covered by ferns, conifers, and strange-looking gingko trees.

Dinosaurs ruled the Earth. From famous kinds like Stegosaurus and Brachiosaurus to lesser-known but fearsome predators like Cryolophosaurus, the Jurassic Period was an amazing time on Earth.

JURASSIC CROSSWORD

Solve the crossword puzzle below by using information about the Jurassic Period.

ACROSS

4. This fast predator may have run as fast as 50 miles per hour

5. Famous dinosaur with a spiked tail

6. This dinosaur is considered one of the first birds

DOWN

1. This dinosaur is famous for its crest

2. This dinosaur also used to be known as the Brontosaurus

3. These types of animals first appeared near the end of the Triassic Period

CRYOLOPHOSAURUS *(cry-oh-loaf-oh-soar-us)*

Cryolophosaurus had a strange, bony crest that stuck out of its head. It probably used this crest to get attention from other members of its species. (Some birds do this, but their crests are made of feathers.) Cryolophosaurus lived in Antarctica, which was much warmer in the Jurassic Period than it is today.

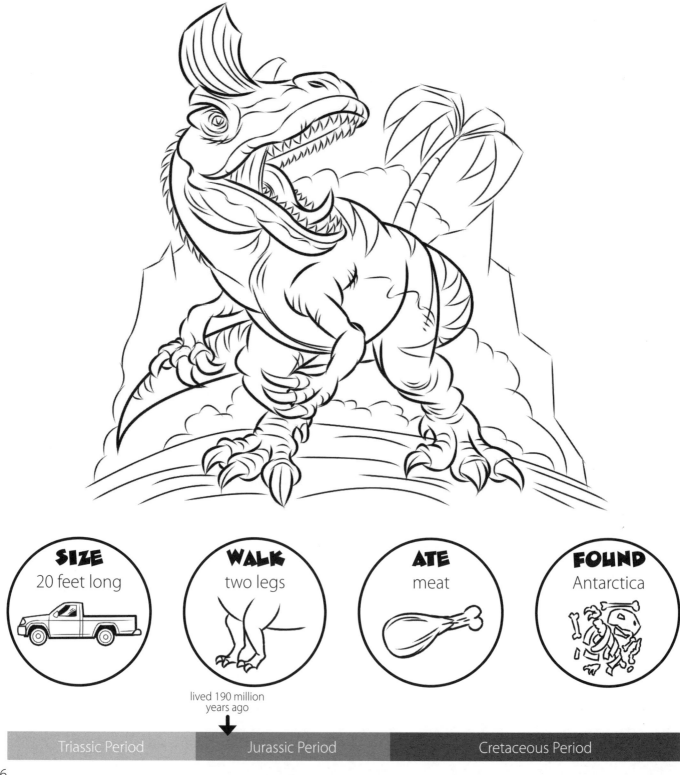

SIZE
20 feet long

WALK
two legs

ATE
meat

FOUND
Antarctica

lived 190 million years ago

| Triassic Period | Jurassic Period | Cretaceous Period |

BRACHIOSAURUS *(brock-ee-oh-soar-us)*

The Brachiosaurus is one of the most famous types of dinosaurs, thanks to its huge size—and its really long neck. Like other sauropods (soar-oh-pods), the Brachiosaurus was huge. These dinosaurs were about as long as two school buses, and they weighed more than 23 cars!

SIZE
70 feet long

WALK
four legs

ATE
plants

FOUND
North America, Africa, Europe

lived 150 million years ago

| Triassic Period | Jurassic Period | Cretaceous Period |

APATOSAURUS *(uh-pat-oh-soar-us)*

Have you ever heard of the Brontosaurus? Scientists used to think Brontosaurus and Apatosaurus were different species. They later learned that the two dinosaurs were the same! Apatosaurus was named first, so scientists use that name. However, some scientists once again believe that the two species were different.

SIZE
70 feet long

WALK
four legs

ATE
plants

FOUND
North America

lived 150 million
years ago

Triassic Period	Jurassic Period	Cretaceous Period

WORD FIND

The nine dinosaur names listed below are hidden in this word puzzle. When you find each name in the puzzle, circle it. Then cross it off the list. Can you find all nine dinosaur species? The words may run forward, backward, up, or down.

```
A S T E G O S A U R U S M L S L
J M V H N O D O N A U G I K C D
T I M E Q F V Q K H E F O G D O
R P J X E Q N G Z Z F I G A H S
O P R H V R M L N O O B A O Z I
O X I O J N U P E P M R E P T F
D R A N T Q V W G N C I V V O E
O P M A N G C P O U H P V D G U
N R Y O F O I K J X V V D L F N
X E R S U R U A S O N N A R Y T
O W N Y T E X G W K P O F Q C E
Q S U R U A S O I H C A R B O I
Y Y A O E I D I P L O D O C U S
O V I R A P T O R I W F F K G C
H A D R O S A U R M T H R T I B
J P H W A A P A T O S A U R U S
```

APATOSAURUS

BRACHIOSAURUS

DIPLODOCUS

HADROSAUR

IGUANODON

OVIRAPTOR

STEGOSAURUS

TROODON

TYRANNOSAURUS REX

THE FIRST MAMMALS

The first mammals appeared toward the end of the Triassic Period, and they lived alongside the dinosaurs in the Jurassic and the Cretaceous periods. Because there were many predators around (including dinosaurs), they had to stay hidden. Color the small mammals in the picture. Are they brightly colored or do they blend in?

DIPLODOCUS (Dip-lodd-uh-cuss)

The Diplodocus was one of the longest animals ever—at times more than 90 feet long. They had a very long tail. Scientists think their tails were used like a whip. If attacked by a meat-eater, a Diplodocus could try to whip the attacker and scare it away. Connect the dots below to see a Diplodocus.

SIZE
90 feet long

WALK
four legs

ATE
plants

FOUND
North and South America, Europe, Africa

lived 150 million years ago

Triassic Period	Jurassic Period	Cretaceous Period

ARCHAEOPTERYX *(arr-kee-op-ter-icks)*

Archaeopteryx is one of the most famous dinosaurs of all time—because it's one of the earliest known bird relatives. How do we know the two groups are related? For one, Archaeopteryx had feathers! So the next time you're at the zoo, take a look at an ostrich or an emu. It's a living Archaeopteryx relative!

SIZE
less than 2 feet

WALK
two legs

ATE
insects/meat

FOUND
Europe

lived 150 million
years ago

Triassic Period	Jurassic Period	Cretaceous Period

STEGOSAURUS *(steg-oh-soar-us)*

The Stegosaurus is one of the most famous dinosaurs, and for good reason. The plates on its back were unique. They looked like armor to protect Stegosaurus from meat-eaters, but scientists think the plates were used to keep the dinosaur cool. The Stegosaurus used sharp tail spikes to defend itself.

SIZE
20 feet long

WALK
four legs

ATE
plants

FOUND
North America

lived 150 million years ago

Triassic Period	Jurassic Period	Cretaceous Period

ALLOSAURUS *(al-oh-soar-us)*

The Allosaurus is one of the most well-known dinosaur species—and it's famous for the same reason as the Tyrannosaurus Rex: It was a large predator. Allosaurus was at the top of its food chain. It used its sharp teeth, strong arms, and claws to hunt large, slow plant-eaters like Stegosaurus and Diplodocus.

SIZE
25 feet long

WALK
two legs

ATE
meat

FOUND
North America, Europe

lived 163 million years ago

Triassic Period	Jurassic Period	Cretaceous Period

ON THE HUNT

The Allosaurus was a fast, strong dinosaur. It used its speed to hunt slower dinosaurs, such as the Stegosaurus. Scientists think the Allosaurus could have reached 50 miles per hour. The Stegosaurus moved closer to seven miles per hour. That would be like a car chasing a person!

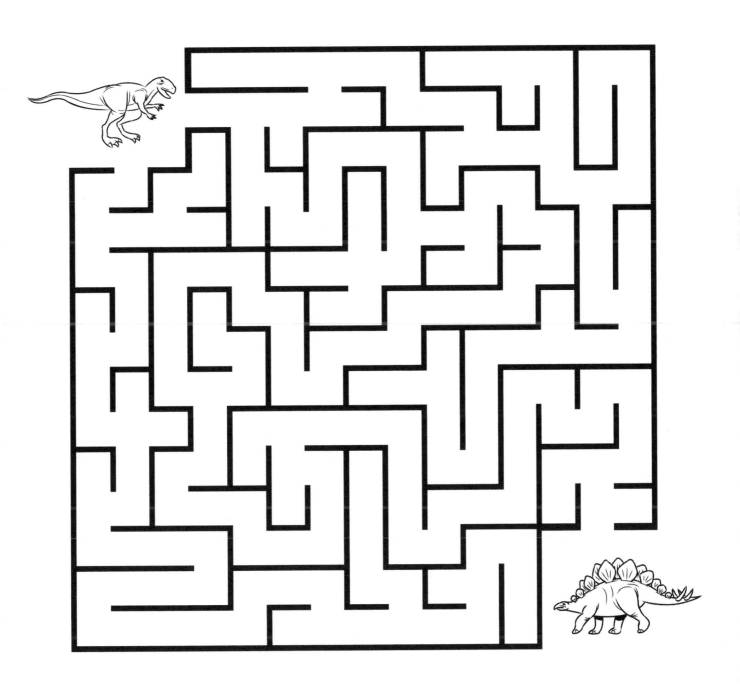

CRETACEOUS PERIOD

(145–65 million years ago)

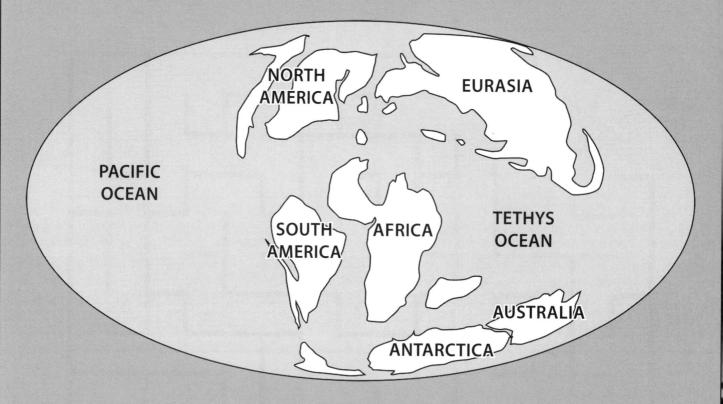

By the end of the Cretaceous Period, the continents were beginning to look more familiar. For instance, North America began to take shape. But an inland sea, called the Western Interior Seaway, split the continent into two pieces: Laramidia (lare-uh-mid-ee-uh) to the west and Appalachia (app-ull-a-chee-uh) to the east.

Dinosaurs continued to rule the land. Large marine creatures hunted in the seas. New creatures and new life forms began to appear. In fact, many insect, mammal, and bird species first lived in the Cretaceous.

The Cretaceous Period may have been a prettier time than the Jurassic Period. That's because the first flowering plants appeared in the Cretaceous.

CRETACEOUS CROSSWORD

Solve the puzzle below by using information about the Cretaceous Period.

ACROSS

1. Famous for its "killing claw"

4. These pretty things didn't exist until the Cretaceous

6. This dinosaur was covered in armor

7. The most famous dinosaur, in short

DOWN

2. The Earth was hit by one of these at the end of the Cretaceous Period

3. Used its three horns for defense

5. We now know that many dinosaurs had these on their bodies

THE FIRST FLOWERS

It might sound strange, but flowers haven't always been around. In fact, flowering plants didn't appear on Earth until the Cretaceous Period. So there weren't any flowers, and there wasn't any fruit! Before that, most of the plants on Earth looked like ferns and pine trees.

TRICERATOPS *(Tri-sare-uh-tops)*

When people think of the Triceratops, they often compare it to the modern-day rhinoceros. Triceratops' three horns were a good defense against predators. The frill around its head looked like a shield, but it was probably also used to help Triceratops cool down. Connect the dots below to see a Triceratops.

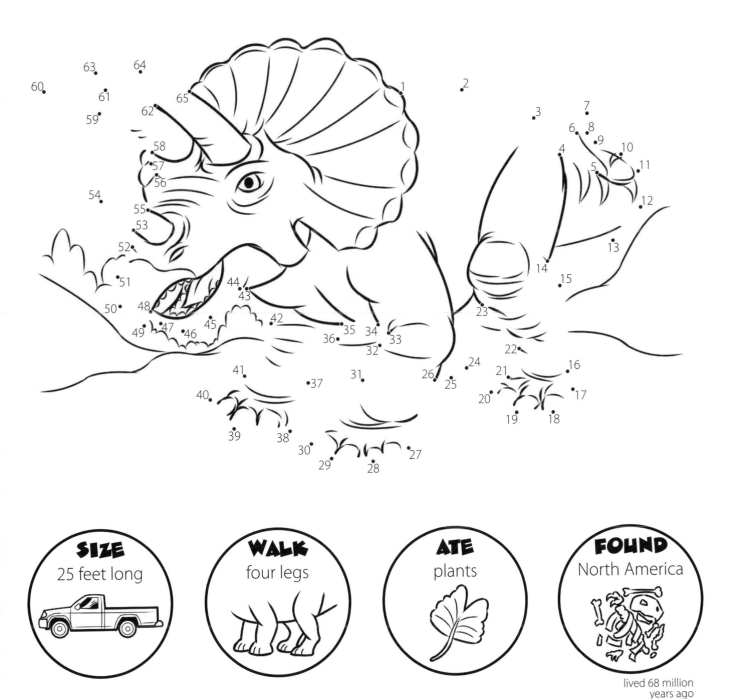

SIZE
25 feet long

WALK
four legs

ATE
plants

FOUND
North America

lived 68 million
years ago

Triassic Period | Jurassic Period | Cretaceous Period

TYRANNOSAURUS REX *(Tie-ran-oh-soar-us rex)*

The Tyrannosaurus Rex is probably the most famous—and the most popular—kind of dinosaur. There's good reason for that. After all, it was a huge, fast predator. It had teeth the size of bananas, and it ruled the land during the Cretaceous Period. The Triceratops was among T. Rex's favorite foods!

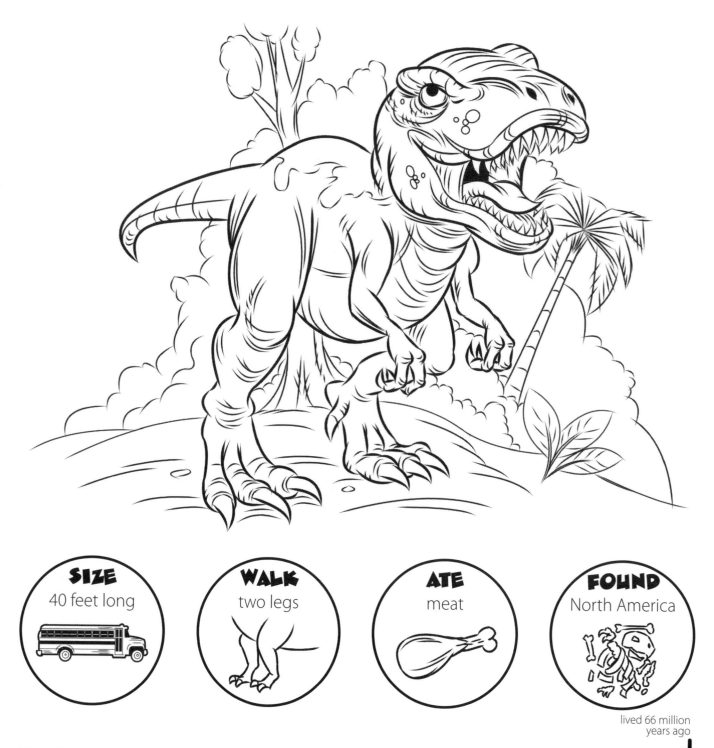

SIZE
40 feet long

WALK
two legs

ATE
meat

FOUND
North America

lived 66 million years ago

Triassic Period	Jurassic Period	Cretaceous Period

VELOCIRAPTOR *(Vell-oss-ih-rap-tur)*

Most people who have heard of Velociraptors tend to think this species was as big as a person. In truth, Velociraptors were closer to the size of a turkey. But these dinosaurs had sharp teeth and could run faster than 35 miles per hour. Plus, they had deadly claws on each foot.

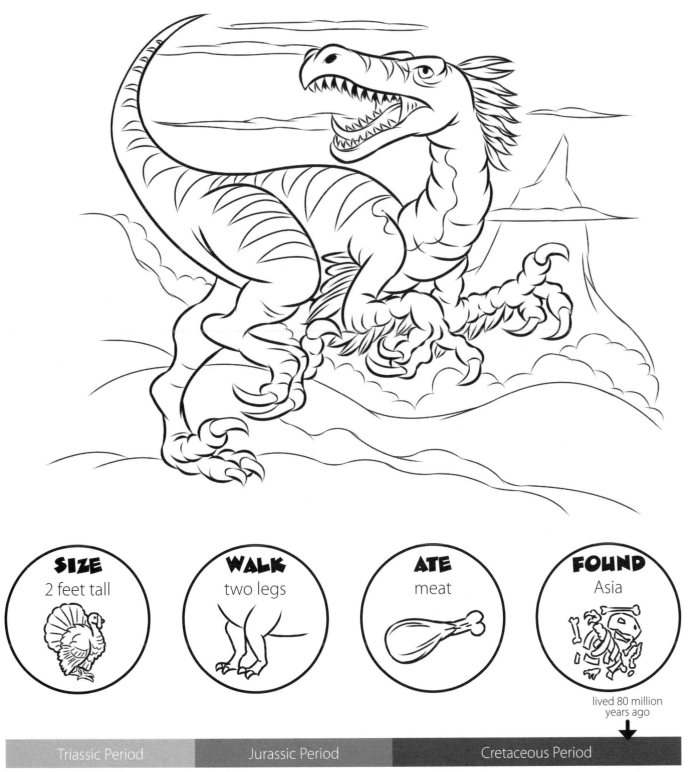

SIZE
2 feet tall

WALK
two legs

ATE
meat

FOUND
Asia

lived 80 million years ago

Triassic Period	Jurassic Period	Cretaceous Period

DINOSAURS WITH FEATHERS!

When scientists first discovered dinosaurs, they thought the creatures were big and slow lizards. In fact, the word "dinosaur" means "fearfully great lizard." Since then, scientists have learned something very surprising: Many dinosaurs had feathers! How do we know? Some dinosaur fossils still have feather imprints!

ACTIVITY: Choose a different dinosaur from this book, and imagine what it might have looked like covered with feathers. Draw it on a separate piece of paper.

FROM DINOSAURS TO BIRDS

Today, we know that dinosaurs weren't really lizards. They share more in common with birds. Follow the maze, and see how dinosaurs slowly evolved, or became birds, over millions of years. Make sure your line goes through each kind of animal.

TROODON *(tro-uh-don)*

The Troodon was a small, fast dinosaur species. It's well-known for one big reason: Troodons had big skulls—and a big skull usually houses a big brain. They were probably very smart dinosaurs. Study the Troodons below. How many things are different in the second Troodon picture?

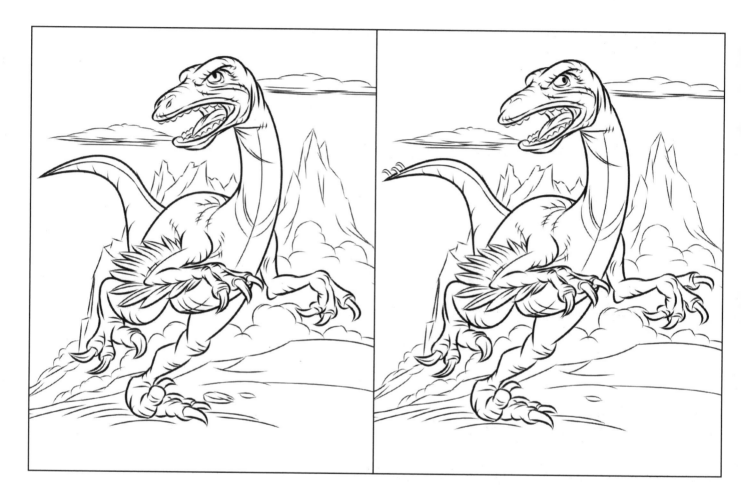

SIZE
7 feet long

WALK
two legs

ATE
meat (& plants)

FOUND
North America, Asia

lived 77 million years ago

Triassic Period	Jurassic Period	Cretaceous Period

OVIRAPTOR *(oh-vuh-rap-tur)*

The Oviraptor's name means "egg snatcher." One of the first Oviraptor fossils was found near a nest of eggs. Scientists thought the Oviraptor had been about to eat the eggs. Since then, Oviraptor fossils have been found sitting on their nests—just like birds do. So the Oviraptor didn't snatch eggs. It protected them!

SIZE
6 feet long

WALK
two legs

ATE
meat

FOUND
North America, Asia

lived 71 million years ago

Triassic Period	Jurassic Period	Cretaceous Period

IGUANODON *(ig-wahn-uh-don)*

One of the first dinosaur species ever discovered, the Iguanodon got its name because scientists thought its teeth resembled those of a giant iguana. This led to the idea that dinosaurs were huge, slow lizards. In fact, the Iguanodon was more similar to a giant cow.

SIZE
25 feet long

WALK
four legs
(sometimes two)

ATE
plants

FOUND
North and South
America, Europe,
Asia, Africa

lived 127 million
years ago

Triassic Period	Jurassic Period	Cretaceous Period

HADROSAUR *(had-row-soar)*

Hadrosaurs were a large group of plant-eating dinosaurs. Hadrosaurs are known as "duck-billed" dinosaurs, thanks to their funny mouths. Many Hadrosaur species also had crests on their heads. Some species' crests were hollow, so their crests may have been used as a type of horn to communicate.

SIZE
20 feet long

WALK
four legs

ATE
plants

FOUND
North and South America, Europe, Asia, Antarctica

lived 71 million years ago

Triassic Period	Jurassic Period	Cretaceous Period

TRICERATOPS HORNS

The Triceratops gets its name from the three horns on its head. Not all relatives of Triceratops had three horns. Some, like Protoceratops, had no horns at all. Other species had more than three horns. Kosmoceratops had more than 15! Draw the other half of the Triceratops picture below.

PARASAUROLOPHUS *(pare-uh-soar-all-uh-fuss)*

Parasaurolophus is a large, plant-eating dinosaur. It's most famous for its tube-like crest atop its head. This hollow crest gave the Parasaurolophus a football-shaped head. The Parasaurolophus probably used its horn-like crest as a way to signal other members of its species.

SIZE
25 feet long

WALK
four legs

ATE
plants

FOUND
North America

lived 72 million years ago

Triassic Period	Jurassic Period	Cretaceous Period

ANKYLOSAURUS *(an-kyle-oh-soar-us)*

The Ankylosaurus was one tough dinosaur. Most of its body was covered in thick, bony armor, and its tail was capped with a dangerous club. Why did Ankylosaurus need all the protection? Because this dinosaur species was a slow plant-eater, which made it easy for big, fast predators to catch.

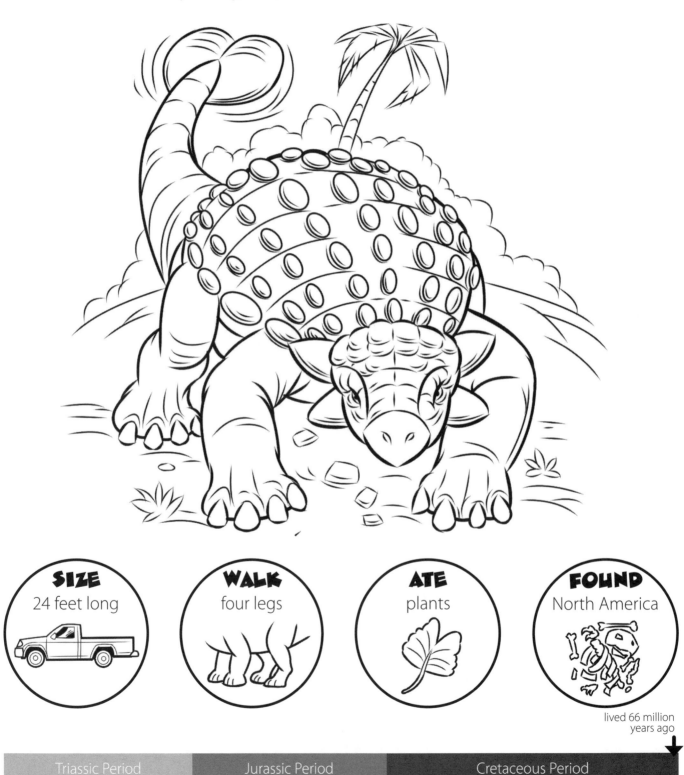

SIZE
24 feet long

WALK
four legs

ATE
plants

FOUND
North America

lived 66 million years ago

Triassic Period	Jurassic Period	Cretaceous Period

DINOSAUR DEFENSES

What did meat-eating dinosaurs like Tyrannosaurus Rex eat? Other dinosaurs! The plant-eaters had to protect themselves. Many of them did so with their own special defenses. Write the name of each dinosaur below. Then describe the defense it used to protect itself. Which defense do you think was the best?

NON-DINOSAURS

Not every creature that lived a long time ago was a dinosaur. The species in this section lived at the same time as dinosaurs, but they weren't dinosaurs. Some soared through the skies, while others were sea monsters that hunted in the oceans. But these creatures evolved from different ancestors, so they aren't quite the same as a dinosaur.

PTERANODON *(Tur-ann-oh-don)*

The Pteranodon belonged to a group of animals called pterosaurs (tare-oh-soars). This species was famous for its long wingspan, up to 20 feet wide. (Bald eagles have wingspans of about seven feet.) The Pteranodon didn't have the biggest wingspan of all pterosaurs, though. Some others had wingspans of 30 feet!

SIZE
6 feet tall

WALK
two legs

ATE
meat (fish)

FOUND
North America

lived 80 million years ago

Triassic Period	Jurassic Period	Cretaceous Period

ICHTHYOSAUR *(ick-tee-oh-soar)*

Ichthyosaurs were a group of creatures that looked like dolphins or fish, but they were reptiles. (Their skeletons were similar to reptiles.) The Ichthyosaur was among the top predators in the oceans. Compared to their body size, they had the largest eyes of any animal, and they probably used them to hunt in dark, deep waters!

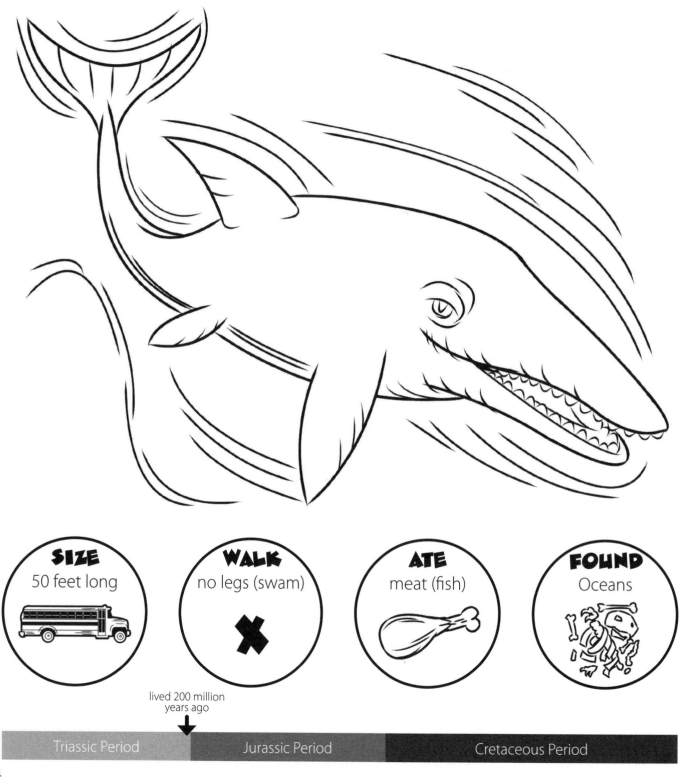

SIZE
50 feet long

WALK
no legs (swam)
✗

ATE
meat (fish)

FOUND
Oceans

lived 200 million
years ago

Triassic Period	Jurassic Period	Cretaceous Period

WORD FIND

The 10 dinosaur and fossil words listed below are hidden in this word puzzle. When you find each word in the puzzle, circle it. Then cross it off the list. Can you find all 10 dinosaur words?

```
L T C F T W R Q P G P K I P
Z J W I H W E C N E I C S C
E Y G O L O T N O E L A P I
D V K F E V K B A E I O U S
G M Y J R U A S A S O M P S
J A T R I A S S I C P L S A
A S V I C H T H Y O S A U R
C E H Y F C V K M J H H K U
O Q S U O E C A T E R C V J
M F Z S C H E P B B N H J O
T J C I O Z O S E M M X M Y
K R U A S O I S E L P C J T
Z A Z D Q X K G A L E L K B
E N D J F S L I S S O F M P
```

CRETACEOUS
FOSSILS
ICHTHYOSAUR
JURASSIC

MESOZOIC
MOSASAUR
PALEONTOLOGY

PLESIOSAUR
SCIENCE
TRIASSIC

PLESIOSAUR *(Plee-see-oh-soar)*

The Plesiosaur was a group of marine reptiles. Many were even bigger than the Ichthyosaur. Some scientists think Plesiosaurs ate squid and other marine reptiles. But fossils have been found with crabs and shells in the stomach area, so maybe Plesiosaurs ate animals on the ocean floor, instead of swimming animals.

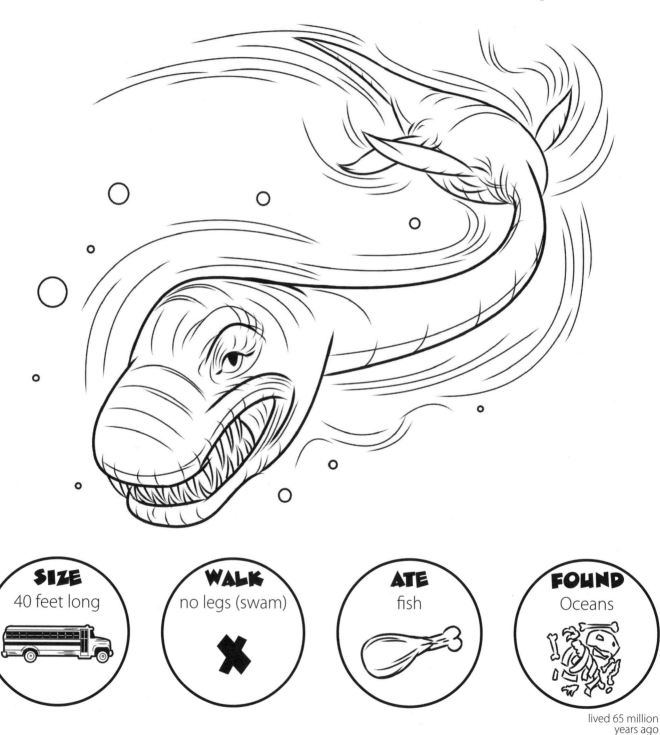

SIZE
40 feet long

WALK
no legs (swam)

ATE
fish

FOUND
Oceans

lived 65 million years ago

Triassic Period   Jurassic Period   Cretaceous Period

MOSASAUR *(Mose-uh-soar)*

The Mosasaur is a group of ocean creatures closely related to lizards. In fact, the Komodo Dragon is one of the Mosasaur's living relatives. During the late Cretaceous Period, the Mosasaur was the top water predator. It was in the ocean what the Tyrannosaurus Rex was on land.

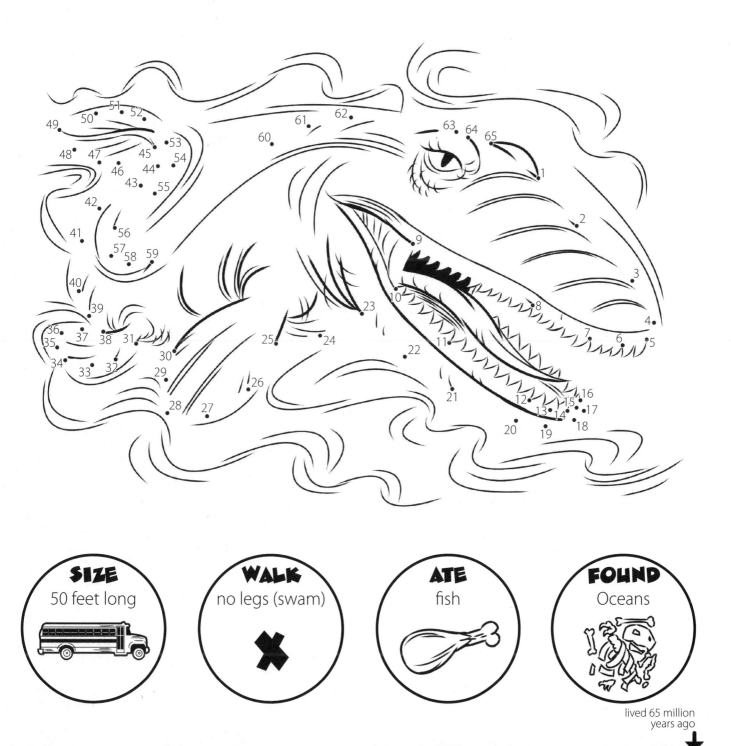

SIZE	WALK	ATE	FOUND
50 feet long	no legs (swam)	fish	Oceans

lived 65 million years ago

Triassic Period | Jurassic Period | Cretaceous Period

PALEONTOLOGY

(pay-lee-un-tall-uh-jee)

People have been finding fossils—including those of dinosaurs—for thousands of years. But for most of history, they didn't know what fossils were or how they formed. Instead, they came up with their own explanations. The huge bones were thought to have come from giants and dragons!

In the past few hundred years, people have learned what fossils really are and how they formed. The study of fossils and other pieces of ancient life is called paleontology. Scientists who study fossils are called paleontologists.

The first famous dinosaur fossils were found in Europe. After that, the dinosaurs of western North America were discovered. Then the search went global. Dinosaur fossils have been found on every continent (even Antarctica), and there are many more dinosaur fossils waiting to be discovered all around the world.

IMPACT EVENT

Dinosaurs ruled the Earth for millions of years, but the last dinosaurs died about 65 million years ago. For a long time, scientists weren't sure why. Now, most believe that the Earth was struck by an asteroid (a giant space rock). The asteroid was six miles wide and hit near present-day Mexico.

FUN FACT! When the asteroid hit, the impact threw a huge amount of dust into the air. It blocked the light of the sun, killing all the plants. The plant-eating dinosaurs had nothing to eat, so they died out. And then the meat-eating dinosaurs had nothing to eat, so they died out, too!

THE FIRST DINOSAUR BONES

For thousands of years, people have known that fossils exist. But before scientists studied the fossils, no one knew where the huge bones came from or what left them behind. Back then, many people thought the bones were from giants and dragons. Yes, even grownups thought giants and dragons were real!

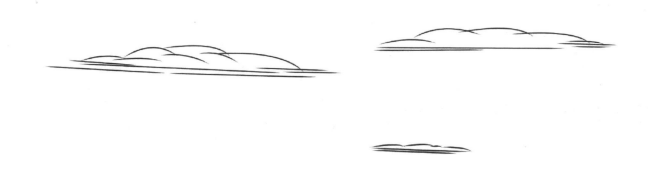

FUN FACT! According to at least one researcher, the discovery of dinosaur fossils led to many famous myths and stories. The researcher pointed out that the Griffin, a famous mythological monster, is a lot like a relative of the Triceratops. Many scientists now agree with her theory.

MARY ANNING

Mary Anning is one of the most important people in the history of paleontology. She helped collect a number of important fossils on the southern coast of England in the early 1800s. Some of her finds included the first Ichthyosaur fossils and the first Plesiosaur fossils. These fossils led many other scientists to look for dinosaur fossils. Help Mary find the fossils and coprolite (fossilized dung) below:

THE BONE WARS

Many of the most important dinosaur fossils were found in North America, by two researchers, during the 1870s. Othniel Marsh and Edward Cope started as friends, but they raced to discover dinosaurs. They soon became enemies in what is now known as the Bone Wars, a contest to see who'd discover the most dinosaurs.

 **FUN FACT!** Neither Cope nor Marsh played fair. They used spies, tried to steal each other's finds, and even used dynamite to prevent each other from finding any fossils. Along the way, they discovered some of the most famous dinosaurs, including Stegosaurus and Triceratops.

LIVING FOSSILS

Dinosaurs survived for millions of years, but some species of animals have lived for much longer. These animals are sometimes called "living fossils." One example is the horseshoe crab. The species has been on Earth for over 400 million years. That's a long time, especially since humans have only been here for two million!

 Despite their name, horseshoe crabs aren't really crabs at all. They are arthropods (arth-row-pods), relatives of scorpions and spiders. You can usually find horseshoe crabs on the East Coast of the United States.

FUN THINGS TO DO

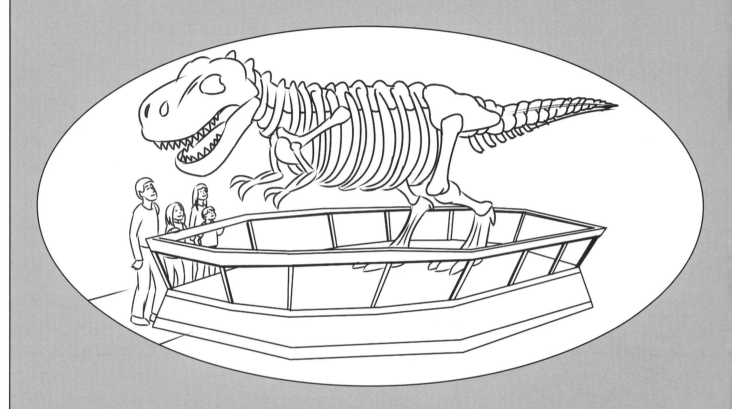

The United States has museums with world-famous dinosaur exhibits and parks where you can see actual dinosaur bones and tracks. Many natural history centers have dinosaur and fossil displays, too. Plus, there are other exciting ways to get involved in the world of paleontology.

Check out this next section, and learn about the adventures that are waiting to be shared by you and your family.

FOSSIL HUNTING

Many important dinosaur fossils are quite rare, so it's against the law to collect them without special permission. But you can still collect other kinds of fossils. In many areas, you can find and keep fossils of invertebrates (animals without a backbone). These kinds of fossils are found in many parts of the country.

You can collect fossils! Ask your parents to help you find a good fossil-hunting area near you. For tips and suggestions, check out a field guide or call your local museum. Then start building your own collection of fossils from the past!

SCIENCE MUSEUM

Do you want to see a real dinosaur fossil? Visit a science museum! Many science museums have dinosaurs on display. It's amazing to walk beside a towering Brachiosaurus or a snarling Tyrannosaurus Rex. Some museums even offer a chance to camp under the dinosaurs! Help the family below get to the museum.

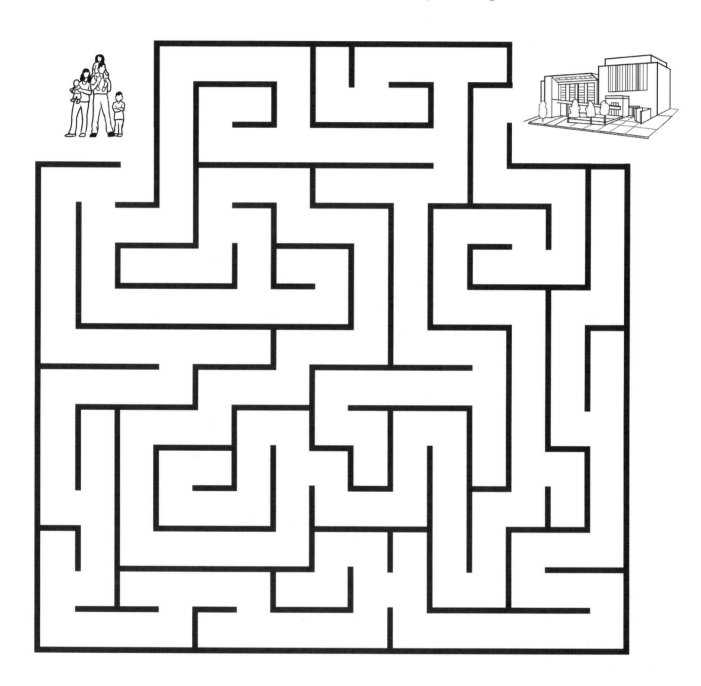

DINOSAUR TRACKS

Dinosaurs left their bones behind, and some also left footprints! Dinosaur tracks are more common than you might guess. Of course, they made footprints when they walked on soft ground—just like you do. Sometimes, the ground got hard, and the footprints eventually fossilized. That's why they can still be seen today.

 Dinosaur fossils only formed under just the right conditions, so they are rare. Dinosaur footprints are more common. You can see dinosaur footprints in places all around the country. Many of these places are in the southern and western United States.

FAVORITE FOODS

When it comes to food, dinosaurs are often divided into two groups: those that ate plants (or herbivores) and those that ate meat (or carnivores). Take a look at the dinosaurs listed below. Write the names of the plant-eaters under the leaf, and write the names of the meat-eaters under the leg bone.

ALLOSAURUS   EORAPTOR   OVIRAPTOR
BRACHIOSAURUS   HADROSAUR   PARASAUROLOPHUS
CRYOLOPHOSAURUS   IGUANODON   STEGOSAURUS
DIPLODOCUS   ODONTOCHELYS   TRICERATOPS

BONUS: Some dinosaurs were omnivores. That means they ate meat and plants (just like most humans do). Which dinosaur in this activity book was noted as both a meat-eater and a plant-eater? Write your answer below:

DINOSAUR JOKES

1. *Which dinosaur species could jump higher than a house?*
   All of them; houses can't jump

2. *What do you call it when a dinosaur gets in a car accident?*
   Tyrannosaurus wreck

3. *What do you call a person who makes clothes for dinosaurs?*
   A dino-sewer

4. *What do you call a Stegosaurus that won't stop talking?*
   A dino-bore

5. *What do you call a blind Cryolophosaurus?*
   Do-you-think-he-saurus

6. *What do you call a blind Cryolophosaurus' dog?*
   Do-you-think-he-saurus Rex

7. *Why do museums have old dinosaur bones?*
   They can't afford new ones

8. *What does Triceratops sit on?*
   Its Tricera-bottom

9. *Why did some dinosaurs eat raw meat?*
   Because they didn't know how to cook

10. *How do you tell if a Brachiosaurus is asleep?*
    Listen for the dino-snores

11. *What's the best way to talk to a Velociraptor?*
    Long distance

12. *What do you get when a dinosaur blows its nose?*
    Out of the way

WHAT'S WRONG WITH THIS?

Sometimes, people think that all dinosaurs lived at the same time. But that's not true. Some famous dinosaurs never even met. The dinosaurs shown below—the Tyrannosaurus Rex and the Stegosaurus—are two of the most famous dinosaurs, but they lived many millions of years apart!

QUIZ YOUR PARENTS

1. The Mesozoic Era is known as the age of dinosaurs, and it's made of three different time periods. Which one of them came first?

     a. Cretaceous Period
     b. Triassic Period
     c. Jurassic Period

2. Which of the following dinosaurs did the Tyrannosaurus Rex eat?

     a. Brachiosaurus
     b. Eoraptor
     c. Stegosaurus
     d. Triceratops

3. Which of the following dinosaurs had strong armor and used its club-like tail to defend itself?

     a. Stegosaurus
     b. Ankylosaurus
     c. Iguanodon
     d. Brachiosaurus

4. Which of the following animals lived around the same time as the dinosaurs but wasn't actually a dinosaur?

     a. Ichthyosaur
     b. Mosasaur
     c. Pteranodon
     d. All of the above

5. When did the first flowering plants appear on Earth?

     a. Cretaceous Period
     b. Triassic Period
     c. Jurassic Period

ANSWERS

PAGE 3—WHAT ARE DINOSAURS?
Birds

PAGE 5—DINOSAUR TIMELINE
Triceratops, it was the only dinosaur alive at the same time as Tyrannosaurus Rex.

PAGE 7—DINOSAUR MATCHING
Iguanodon = Ornithopod
Triceratops = Ceratopsian
Stegosaurus = Stegosaur
Tyrannosaurus Rex = Theropod
Ankylosaurus = Ankylosaur

PAGE 9—TRIASSIC CROSSWORD

PAGE 10—BEFORE THE DINOSAURS
Prestosuchus (press-toe-soo-kuss)

PAGE 13—DINOSAUR SIZES
1. Eoraptor; 2. Car; 3. Prestosuchus;
4. Elephant; 5. Tyrannosaurus Rex;
6. Brachiosaurus; 7. Skyscraper

PAGE 15—JURASSIC CROSSWORD
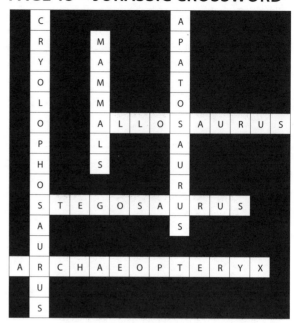

PAGE 19—WORD FIND
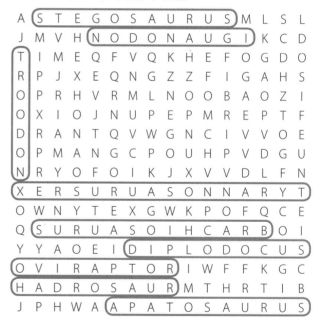

PAGE 20—THE FIRST MAMMALS
They should blend in to help them hide from meat-eaters.

ANSWERS

PAGE 25—ON THE HUNT

PAGE 33—FROM DINOSAURS TO BIRDS

PAGE 27—CRETACEOUS CROSSWORD

PAGE 34—TROODON

Eye looking a different way, nose missing, tooth missing, tail spikes, extra finger on left hand, rock by foot missing

PAGE 41—DINOSAUR DEFENSES

Stegosaurus = tail spikes
Brachiosaurus = large size
Triceratops = horns
Ankylosaurus = armor and tail club

PAGE 45—WORD FIND

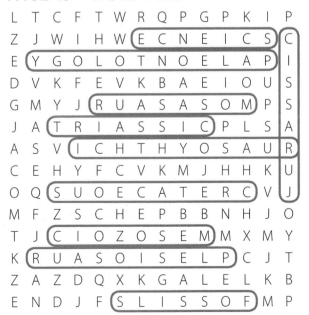

ANSWERS

PAGE 51—MARY ANNING

PAGE 56—SCIENCE MUSEUM

PAGE 58—FAVORITE FOODS

Plants: Brachiosaurus, Diplodocus, Hadrosaur, Iguanodon, Parasaurolophus, Stegosaurus, Triceratops. **Meat:** Allosaurus, Cryolophosaurus, Eoraptor, Odontochelys, Oviraptor. **Omnivore:** Troodon

PAGE 61—QUIZ YOUR PARENTS

1. Triassic Period; 2. Triceratops;
3. Ankylosaurus; 4. All of the above;
5. Cretaceous Period

BOOKS TO READ

Dixon, Douglas. *The Complete Illustrated Encyclopedia of Dinosaurs & Prehistoric Creatures: The Ultimate Illustrated Reference Guide to 1000 Dinosaurs and Prehistoric Creatures*. Southwater: 2014.

Gee, Henry. *A Field Guide to Dinosaurs: The Essential Handbook for Travelers in the Mesozoic*. Chartwell: 2012.

Holtz, Thomas. *Dinosaurs: The Most Complete, Up-to-Date Encyclopedia for Dinosaur Lovers of All Ages*. Random House, 2007.

Mayor, Adrienne. *The Griffin and the Dinosaur: How Adrienne Mayor Discovered a Fascinating Link Between Myth and Science*. National Geographic Books, 2014.

Books Consulted for Fact-Checking

Fastovsky, David. *Dinosaurs: A Concise Natural History*. Cambridge University Press, 2009.

Paul, Gregory S. *The Princeton Field Guide to Dinosaurs*. Princeton University Press, 2010.